A Tennessee Soldier

To Carol Hall,

I'm very thankful the Lord allowed our paths to meet. Continue the Lord's work and live fearlessly.

God bless,

Fred C. Min

A Tennessee Soldier

Memoirs of Service in Operation Iraqi Freedom III

FRED C. MIZE III

DEDICATION

To my son Isaiah Mize, who's sacrifice was greater than mine. You endured so much as a six, seven, and eight-year-old boy when I deployed. Thank you, son, for your sacrifice and now for your service as a fellow Tennessee Army National Guard Soldier.

I'm proud of the man, husband, father, and Soldier that you've become.

Love, Dad

Isaiah before and after my return home, 2004-2005

Isaiah's enlistment ceremony on **26 November 2014**

Father and Son, Brothers-in-Arms

TABLE OF CONTENTS

I pray that the LORD blesses you as He did me while I placed my memories into written word. I pray that the LORD blesses you with not only giving you the wisdom to learn your God given talents but to have the courage to use them for His glory.

ACKNOWLEDGMENTS

To all the brave Tennessee Soldiers of the 278TH Regimental Combat Team who served together, throughout Operation Iraqi Freedom III in 2004-2005.

And so, it begins…

RESPECT

I can still hear the soft-spoken words of my Grandfather, Charles Hobby, telling me prior to shipping to Basic Combat Training to "Speak softly and carry a big stick" and the advice from my Uncle, Kenny Mize, to "Never let them see me sweat". All throughout my years of service I've reflected on those two simple lines of wisdom from my loving family. I've never been a man of large stature nor have I ever been a man of many words. I attribute my slender build to God's design and the few words due to the wisdom bestowed to me from my Grandfather.

Funny memory but the nickname I was given in Basic was "Mouse" due to being both small and quiet. When my comrades made the conclusion that I was a Christian they began calling me "Church Mouse". Twenty years later, I still chuckle at that. Needless to say, one wouldn't think that a soft-spoken man of small stature who was once known as "Church Mouse" would ever be highly respected in the military world that's full of Type A personalities but that wasn't the case.

From being a man of few words, I quickly became known as being a man of action and determination. I attribute this to the wisdom of my Uncle Kenny reminding me, to never let them see me sweat. His words pushed me past my personal limits when my body told me to quit, my heart wouldn't let me because I never wanted anyone or anything to break me down or stop me from doing whatever had to be done.

Have you ever thought how ironic it is that the loudest people are the ones who are rarely heard? I've seen this time and time again along with, those who complain the most receive the least amount of sympathy. I'll always be thankful for the people God chose to surround me with throughout my life, especially my family who took time to teach me what they learned the hard way in hopes that I wouldn't have to.

Being a Christian while serving in the military hasn't always been easy but like so many things in life that aren't easy are worth the struggles. I first learned this as a young Private First Class at Fort Sill, Oklahoma, striving to graduate Basic Combat Training and Advance Individual Training to become a Field Artillerymen. Like all who've served, I'll never forget my Drill Sergeant. Drill Sergeant Shields was a tall 6'5" man who was literally, lean and mean. He never cracked a smile and said the Lord's name in vain often. During one formation, Drill Sergeant Shields asked my platoon if it bothered any of us when he'd say, "GD". I know I wasn't the only one it bothered but we were all scared to speak up and say anything. I mean really, what Private in their right mind would want to confront a Drill Sergeant? I felt so pathetic to not stand up for God and tell Drill Sergeant Shields that it did in fact offend me because I knew it offended God. That sense of letting God down lit a small flame within me.

A week later while addressing our Platoon in formation, Drill Sergeant Shields asked us once again if him saying "GD" bothered anyone. That small flame within me grew to a raging inferno as all 116 lbs. of me, stood in the midst of my fellow soldiers, raised my right hand and said, "Drill Sergeant, yes, hearing you take God's name in vain does offend me because it offends Him, Drill Sergeant". I knew I didn't want to stand up to Drill Sergeant Shields but even more so I didn't want to let God down as I did before. I was shocked that Drill Sergeant Shields didn't punish me for doing what I did but it was obvious to all of my platoon, that he expected more from me than the others I served with from that moment on, until I graduated Advanced Individual Training and left Fort Sill, Ok.

Years later in 2004 while training at Camp Shelby, MS in preparation for Operation Iraqi Freedom III, my brothers-in-arms coined me with a new nickname which I still carry today. My last name of "Mize" is just four letters long but mispronounced so often. The cadre assigned as our instructors mispronounced it badly with their long southern drawl during every roll call. I answered, "here Sergeant" to everything from Mice, Mess, Mees, to even Mizer. My best friend Sergeant Berry, AKA Brother Berry, found this so comical that out of the blue he called me Meeso. My closest friends still refer to me as such.

Months later while conducting precombat checks on our M109A6 Paladin with my gun crew in the motor pool of Camp Buehring, Kuwait, we received horrible news. Our Battery First Sergeant stated that he was reassigning our Paladin to a different gun crew. Now, imagine being told by the same man six months prior that our assigned gun at that time would be the gun we'd go to war with, so get to know her like the back of your hands. That we did. We not only trained and perfected our crew drills on that Paladin but we learned all of her strengths, weaknesses and capabilities. She became a fine-tuned machine and we, her crew, gave her life. We were confident to take her into battle and now just a day prior to crossing the Iraq border we were being told that she was being transferred to another crew and we'd be assigned a gun we knew nothing about. My crew became enraged, rightfully so.

I knew I had to do something and quick to distract them from taking action into their own hands. I knew them even better than our beloved gun so I knew that our First Sergeant was about to receive serious bodily harm if I couldn't calm their nerves. What was a young, Sergeant of small stature and calm demeanor to do? Smoke a cigarette of course...

Surrounded by my beloved brothers I asked for a cigarette. Being a man whom they've never seen smoke, drunk, and strive to not curse was asking for a cigarette. Everyone got quiet and still as Sergeant James pulled a cigarette from his pack and watched me reach for it along with his lighter. I stood there on the sands of Kuwait, surrounded by my brothers and smoked my first and only cigarette. Once my smoke was finished our crew's anger was subsided at least to the point that we calmly talked our First Sergeant from enforcing his radical decision and we went to war in our cherished gun.

Weeks later after several hours in the hot Iraq sun I was refreshed by walking into Forward Operation Base

Caldwell's Dining Facility (DFAC). The DFAC was full of soldiers standing in line with trays in hand while many were already enjoying their chow. As I walked to a table with at least thirty of my comrades who were already eating, talking, and even laughing, I sat down alongside Brother Berry and bowed my head to give thanks to God for my meal and health. The instant that my hands were crossed and head bowed everyone at our table grew silent. Not one word was spoken, the laughter ceased, and eating stopped. Once I said amen and raised my head everything continued as if a play button was pressed after being paused. I never asked my brothers to do this. No one orchestrated it to take place. Each of them respected me enough to allow me to give thanks to God while being surrounded by silence.

I say all of this because to be respected, truly respected not because of your authority or position but for who you are, I've learned that often you're respected for not just what you do but even for what you don't do. As a Christian Soldier always be willing to stand up for your beliefs, even to a Drill Sergeant. Strive to live as Jesus Christ desires you to but be the first to admit your faults, failures, and sins because you'll never be perfect in this life and those who are watching you will respect you all the more for it. They may even love and respect you enough to coin you with nicknames such as, Church Mouse or Meeso.

Drill Sergeant Shields

Myself "PFC Mize" in Basic Combat Training, 13 OCT 00

Camp Buehring, Kuwait before crossing into Iraq, 2004

Top Left to Right: SPC Brad Walker, SPC Brandon Welch, SPC Jonathan Harrison, SGT Carl James, SGT Jason "Brother" Berry, SSG Robert Price "Chief"

Bottom Left to Right: SGT "G" Reynaldo Gutierrez Jr., SGT Fred Mize III, SPC Von Reagan

ACCEPTING TO DIE

For every Soldier it's different. When the first Soldiers prepared for battle, they prepared not just their bodies and their skills but just as importantly they prepared their minds for the unknown. The vast unknown. Regardless of the thousands of years that separated those Soldiers to the Soldiers of today the same questions filled their minds then as they do now. Will I fight honorably? Will I be killed? Will I be captured? Will I be injured? Will I end someone's life? What will my life be like after this battle, after this war? Will my family understand? Will my family still love and respect me? Is it a sin to kill in war? Why am I doing this?

No matter how fit or skilled a Soldier is, if they aren't prepared mentally for battle, they will not succeed and may not survive. As I've already stated, every Soldier prepares for battle in their own way. I can only now explain how I prepared.

I was blessed to not worry about death, for death lost its sting for me when I was just nine years old. As a young boy I accepted Jesus Christ as my Lord and Savior. Although I have failed him every day since then, He has never failed me. He gave me comfort as I prepared my mind for war in knowing that if I gave my life for my country in battle that I'd live eternally with Him not for anything I've done but for Him giving His life for my salvation.

I did not want to die in 2004-2005 while serving in Operation Iraqi Freedom III. At that time, I was still a young man of twenty-seven and a father of a six-year-old son who I desired deeply to see grow into a fine man. Although I was prepared to die, I desired to live. I prepared to live by accepting to die. To many this may seem odd to be prepared to live by accepting to die but that's exactly what I did. Before I crossed the Iraq border, I had already accepted to die in Iraq. Although I had thoughts of returning home, I always followed those thoughts with thoughts of not returning. Every night before I slept, I accepted not waking. Every morning when I woke, I thanked God for that new day and accepted that it may be my last. This may seem morbid to many but for me it became a normal train of thought. I simply, fully accepted dying in Iraq.

I believe this effectively prepared me for the unknown during times of extreme stress of; almost being decapitated by a wire cable guerrilla attack, conducting personnel and vehicle searches, providing checkpoint security checks, mounted and dismounted patrols, volunteering for route clearance missions, and by being on the receiving end of mortar and AK-47 fire. The power of this mindset allowed me to remain focused on the Soldier tasks at hand rather than clouding my mind with thoughts of staying alive. Due to reacting to these situations without any unnecessary hesitations allowed me to share this with you today. As ironic as it may sound, accepting to die kept me alive. I was fully mentally prepared for battle but unprepared mentally for coming back home.

Once my tour of duty in Iraq was over, I remember looking out my window staring down to the Atlantic Ocean on the long eighteen-hour flight thinking of; am I really going home right now? What am I going to say to my family? Will things be as they were before I left? Will they view me differently? Will they understand? Why am I so nervous?

When I saw my son Isaiah, who was six when I left and eight when I returned, joy filled my heart as I wrapped my arms around him while he cried, "Daddy!" I felt on top of the world to be in the presence of my family again and I'm sure this was evident on the outside although I was in turmoil on the inside. I was so emotionally torn in so many ways. I was thankful to be with my family but I missed my brothers-in-arms. I felt at peace at home but more alive in Iraq. I felt guilty for being so blessed. I felt guilty for being home. I felt very, very alone even when I was surrounded by family. The only time I didn't feel alone was when I was with my best friend SGT Jason Berry, AKA "Brother Berry" whom I served in Iraq with. So many strange things bothered me; people complaining about things like money, bills, the weather, where to eat or what to wear. I was also bothered by strange things like people wasting food, being in crowds, car horns, trash or dead animals on the side of the road, and even seeing people smile in church.

Nine years of harboring these emotions and covering up or avoiding their triggers began to take a heavy toil in my life. I wanted to receive professional help but was concerned for being placed on medication that may only mask the problems. I was also concerned that if I was diagnosed with and treated for post-traumatic stress disorder (PTSD) that my military career would come to a premature end.

In countless ways God has directed my path in life and me getting help for PTSD was no different. In 2013 I was conducting a recruiting display at Jefferson County High School. Which is the high school I graduated from in 1996. My former guidance counselor Mr. Bruce Davenport stopped by my display and asked, "How I was doing and how was my military career coming along?" It was easy for me to talk with Bruce then, just as it was when I was a student there seventeen years earlier. I explained how I enjoyed serving as a Soldier but continued to share with him about the alarmingly high suicide rate among service members. Bruce being the caring person he is asked if he could come by my office at the Jefferson City Armory so that we could discuss how he may be able to help prevent Soldiers from making that tragic decision.

Within a week Bruce and I met at my office and he explained to me about Choice Theory Psychology and asked if I'd be willing to speak to his Psychology students at Carson-Newman College about why I felt that suicide rates are so high in the military. I agreed to speak to his students and while I was sharing with them and Bruce why I felt Soldiers choose to commit suicide, I opened up unexpectedly and shared some of my experiences in Iraq and how those experiences made me feel as they happened and how I felt at that point in my life.

Although I have never had thoughts of committing suicide there have been several moments in my life that I got down on my hands and knees and begged God to end my life.

All of those moments were after my service in Iraq because of how I'd feel alone, isolated, angry, sad, misunderstood, unaccepted and broken. Most of these emotions would last for just a few minutes or days but at times for months without ceasing. The only time I'd feel normal was when I was visiting with veterans whom I served with. Any other time I felt as though my emotions controlled me verses me controlling my emotions. I shared that this must be what other Soldiers were experiencing and was either afraid to get help or thought that there wasn't any help for them so they turned to suicide.

After that meeting with Bruce's Phycology class, he began voluntarily coming to my office twice a week and taught me more about Choice Theory in order to help me with the apparent need for help I was crying out for without realizing it. The main PTSD trigger he focused on helping me with was the sound of car horns. I'll share the Iraq experience that led to that trigger in another story.

God blesses everyone with special talents and I believe God's given talent to Bruce is his genuine compassion and empathy to listen to people's unique needs and an overwhelming desire to help them anyway he can. Out of the kindness of his heart Bruce volunteered his time and energy to help me over come so many effects of PTSD to the point that I felt free again. On Veterans Day in 2014 I being a combat veteran reached out to Bruce and thanked him for giving me my freedom back. No matter who you are or what you do for a living, you have God given talents. Use your talents to selflessly help others.

Matthew 22:36-39

36 Master, which is the great commandment in the law?

37 Jesus said unto him, Thou shalt love the Lord thy God with all thy heart, and with all thy soul, and with all thy mind.

38 This is the first and great commandment.

39 And the second is like unto it. Thou shalt love thy neighbor as Thyself.

Bruce Davenport is a living embodiment of Jesus Christ's desire for mankind to love our neighbors as ourselves. The world needs more people like him. If you are a veteran or someone who has never served in the military but suffer from PTSD, I encourage you to speak to someone and get the help you need. Your life is worth living and you should live every moment to its fullest. Stop letting your yesterday steal your today and tomorrow.

THE LITTLE GIRL

As I sat at my home office desk pondering on what the Lord may lead me to write in my first column in the Morgan County Today (which led to the creation of this book), I caught myself glancing to the collage of photos taken while serving in Howitzer Battery 1ST Squadron 278TH Regimental Combat Team, during my tour of duty in Operation Iraqi Freedom III, in 2004-2005. My eyes are drawn as they are always drawn to the center photo of the collage. It's a simple 3"x5" photo taken of a little girl that's forever burned into my memory. As I think back to the moment that I saw this little girl I can almost smell and feel the Iraq air on my skin.

Imagine if you will, traveling through Iraq in a ground convoy of seventy-two military vehicles. Knowing and accepting that everyone you see could be your enemy who longed to kill you. Yet, you're somehow calm and confident because of the training you've conducted and the faith you have in your Gun Chief, (Staff Sergeant Bob Price) serving alongside you but above all you're calm because of your faith in Jesus Christ being your Savior. Knowing that if all the men serving beside you fell, you would not be alone. Knowing that even if you're taken captive as a prison of war, you would not be alone. All because Jesus Christ would always be with you.

That is the confidence and the calmness I served with every day and I believe that's why I made it back home.

The first day of your three-day convoy finally comes to an end and your convoy takes refuge for the night in Scania Iraq. When you and SSG Price, AKA Chief, wakes up the next morning several Soldiers in the surrounding vehicles ask, "if we heard it all last night?" We asked, "heard what"? And they laugh and explain that three mortar rounds came in and hit next to our M109A6 Paladin. Now for those who aren't familiar with the M109A6 Paladin it's a 63,615 lbs. turreted self-propelled howitzer, armed with a 20' 155 mm cannon and the options between a Mk 19 grenade launcher or M2 .50 caliber machine gun. Ours at the time was equipped with a Mk19. I clearly remember Chief and I laughing as the Soldiers spoke because we slept like newborn babies that night and didn't hear a thing out of the norm because our norm consisted of hearing explosions from firing our assortment of lethal artillery rounds for months leading up to our arrival to Iraq. After the Soldiers left our Paladin, I walked around looking at the American might that surrounded me and then I saw several young children mostly shoeless playing with a ball in a small desert field surrounded by razor wire. Moments such as this reminded me that I was no longer in the land I love. No longer in East Tennessee but I was in a foreign land. A completely different world and these shoeless children with futures as inadequate as the clothes on their backs would be a reminder of why I was there. Moments later I watched those young Iraqi children fade into the desert horizon as our convoy continued its mission heading further north into Iraq.

Several hours later our convoy came to a sudden halt as we were traveling at the top speed of the slowest vehicle in our convoy heading toward our destination of Forward Operation Base (FOB) Caldwell. Our senses were heightened as we continuously combed our sectors of fire for a possible ambush while we sat motionless on the main supply route (MSR). Close to an hour had passed but it seemed more like an eternity because with every passing minute the likelihood of an ambush grew. Chief and I finally received a situation report (SITREP) explaining that the convoy was halted because one of our M998 High Mobility Multipurpose Wheeled Vehicles (HMMWV) AKA Humvee and its trailer had jackknifed after taking evasive action. I'll never forget the moment I learned the cause of the accident because it ingrained in me on my second day in country not only how ruthless our enemy was but also how desperate the civilians had become.

The accident was caused by an unthinkable, incomprehensible act of financial desperation or of sheer greed. This act still to this day fifteen years later upsets me but I'll share it with you now. The Iraqi children looked at us with awe and amazement as if we were astronauts from an unknown world rather than U.S. Soldiers riding in armored vehicles while clad in desert camouflage, body armor, and armed with never before seen weaponry.

Imagine now a young five-year-old boy watching with amazement alongside his father as though he was watching a parade for the first time as our convoy cruised across the MSR. Then, without warning and without remorse his father picked him up by the back of his traditional Arabic clothing known as a Kaftan and threw him into the path of our convoy hoping that his son would be killed and he would be compensated by the United States Army for his loss. Needless to say, his child was not killed and he was never paid. I still have disgust in my soul over those snake level low actions and have never experienced a parade with the same joy as prior to that event. Even now with every glance of joyous children rushing for candy being thrown by parade participants, I imagine that innocent little boy.

Once the child was cared for and the father's actions were addressed, we continued mission once again. The desert terrain with every passing mile grew more vast, lifeless, desolate, and bleak. Then I saw her and my heart fell to my boots and my body ached for not being able to act with nothing more than making eye contact with her as we passed leaving her behind. I can't get her memory out of my mind and I pray for her often hoping that she's alive and well. She should now be around nineteen or twenty years old but on that day, she was a young four to five-year-old little girl. All alone in the middle of nowhere along the MSR. She just stood motionless in her torn, sand soaked clothing, and matted hair, not making a sound, not a single movement other than holding her little hand up to her mouth with her fingertips pointed and pressed against her sun cracked lips, signaling that she was hungry and asking for food.

We all knew what our training taught us of how the insurgency used children as bait to pull at American Soldiers' hearts and would unremorsefully sacrifice the children in any desperate attempt to kill even one American Soldier. We knew that we could not stop to give the little girl food, water, or take her with us because our enemy would want nothing more but for our massive convoy to stop so that they would be able to capitalize on our love for children and our moment of compassion by striking at us with their weapon of choice, Improvised Explosive Devices (IEDs) AKA roadside bombs.

I see that little girl every time I eat a meal and think of her as my belly is filled. I can't waste any food to this day and am thankful for never knowing the pain of hunger and such desperation as that precious, innocent little girl had sadly known. I pray Lord, that you bless her life, give her salvation, comfort, absolute joy, and never allow her to know hunger in such a way again as long as she may live.

Children of Scania, Iraq

The Little Girl

DAY THREE

As Chief and I completed our pre-combat checks, thoughts from the past few days freshly filled my mind but the wonder of what this new day held before us, began to take priority. Our convoy had now completed two-thirds of its quest from Camp Buehring in Udari, Kuwait to our destination of Forward Operation Base (FOB) Caldwell located 70 miles east of Baghdad, Iraq. What would we face today; roadside bombs, car bombs, small arms fire, vehicle rollover? The only thing we knew for certain was that whatever laid before us we had each other's backs and would face it together. Intense exhilaration fueled our spirits just as the roar of our convoy's diesel engines filled the brisk desert morning air as our massive convoy rolled out toward FOB Caldwell. Day three had begun.

Our convoy security M998 (HUMVEE) Gun trucks kept civilian vehicles from entering the ranks among our vehicles. Deadly UH-64 Apache Attack Helicopters provided security from above and casted fear into our enemy by diving down to just inches above the ground. M2 Bradley Fighting Vehicles scanned the horizon with their 25 mm M242 Bushmaster chain guns. Indestructible M1 Abram Tanks cowered the enemy with their powerful 120 mm guns. Chief scanned his sector of fire on our right flank while manning the Mk-19 grenade launcher mounted at our Paladin's Gun

Chief's hatch while I scanned my sector of fire on our left flank from the Gunner's hatch with my M-4 rifle and AT4 rocket launcher. Every Tennessee Army National Guard Soldier, in every vehicle was prepared and ready to fight and we were honored to be among them.

Throughout our convoy operation we were reminded how President George W. Bush rallied our Nation's allies to help us fight in the Global War Against Terrorism after 9/11. We saw Japanese Soldiers patrolling the main supply route (MSR) in their dark olive drab compact gun trucks, crossed a Tigris River bridge secured by Italian Soldiers, and drove through a convoy check point manned by laid back comfortably dressed Australian Soldiers wearing khaki shorts, bonnie caps and no body armor. Oh, how I envied them at that moment.

By midday the convoy hadn't encountered any resistance and it appeared that we may make it to FOB Caldwell and finish the day's mission without incident. Our enemy would be foolish to attack such an overwhelming force of firepower and might but we weren't fighting a conventional uniformed enemy. We were fighting an insurgency who fought like snakes hidden deep within blades of grass. I had no respect for the Iraqi insurgency.

Long before my combat boots made their first print in Iraq sand, I accepted knowing that I may have to take another man's life for my country, for the heinous acts of 9/11, to ensure freedom and peace for my family and future generations. I was not haunted by that realization but I was troubled with the thought of ending a man's life and sending him to Hell prior to him accepting Jesus Christ as their Lord and Savior.

I'll never forget standing in wait for any type of attack and praying not for my own life to be spared but for my enemies' salvation prior to me ending his.

Just as the desert sky gained its amber hew with the day's setting sun, we saw the city of Baqubah approaching on the horizon. Our vehicles tightened the gap between intervals as the roadway narrowed once we entered the desert city. An uneasiness came upon me as I made eye contact with the souls living within its gates. Was it the setting sun that caused this uneasy feeling within me or was it something more?

Scanning left to right, preparing to react to anything, thinking of completing this mission, listening to radio chatter, scanning again left to right, then I see it… a thick cable, much like a powerline, arose out of the road just ahead of our Paladin. I yelled, "Chief, Chief, Chief!" Before I could utter another word, the cable had crossed over our gun's 20' cannon, shoved my M-4 rifle into my individual body armor (IBA), and wrapped across Chief's Mk-19 grenade launcher mount. Our convoy never slowed as our Paladin's momentum took hold of the cable and tore it from its braces being held by two adjacent buildings.

Silence… broken by "Chief, are you okay?" "Yes, you?" "I'm good, Chief". Once we realized we were both okay again silence took place for about a mile then sounds of relief, thankfulness and anger filled our Paladin's comms as we talked about how well the insurgents hid and timed the cable for its duty. They were only off by a few inches by judging the distance needed to align the cable to tighten just above Chief's Mk-19. If not for their slight error, you would not be reading about my third day in Operation Iraqi Freedom III, much less had ever known my name. But that wasn't the end. That wasn't our time. It was only, day three.

AH-64 Apache Attack Helicopter on patrol

Tigris river bridge crossing guarded by Italian Soldiers

MUDDY

According to the American Veterinary Medical Association, www.avma.org, 36% of U.S. households own a dog. That's a whopping 43,346,000 households. Sadly, we all know that all of those households don't treat their dogs with love as though they were family. If I was to make an educated guess, I'd say that most are treated with love, just as though they were family. Here in the East Tennessee area alone we celebrate our companionship with dogs by enjoying parades and festivals in their honor and show our respect for the sacrifices of military and law enforcement dogs by giving them rank and service medals. According to www.military. com, "K9 Veterans Day, March 13th is a day set aside to honor the service and sacrifices of military service and working dogs throughout history".

My first hand experiences in Iraq taught me in a quick hurry that women and children weren't treated or viewed anywhere close to how we as Americans treat or view them. Sadly, I found this to also be true for how the average Iraqi treated dogs. Out of all the homes and vehicles I searched I never saw a single dog treated as a pet with even the slightest amount of love. All the dogs I saw were owned and used for a single purpose which was for security and let me say, dogs served that purpose well.

With all of our technology, training and discipline pertaining to both noise and light while conducting night dismounted foot patrol missions, dogs always gave away our positions. This became predominantly clear to me while conducting a dismounted patrol at approximately 2100 in the village of El Mansouria, Iraq. As we dismounted our three M998 "Humvee" Gun Trucks and one Bradley Infantry Fighting Vehicle to embark on the patrol I remember looking up into the moonless night sky while wearing my night vision goggles and seeing an AH-64 Apache attack helicopter overseeing our mission from above. I felt good knowing that our movements and status were being watched from above and by the Soldiers who manned the Bradley's mighty 25 mm M242 Bushmaster chain gun and BGM-71 TOW anti-tank missile. We felt confident that we would complete our mission successfully due to our advanced training, technology, and discipline.

Approximately twenty minutes of silent movements in the moonless night our patrol mission was compromised due to a dog picking up our scent and giving away our position. All of our training, technology, and discipline was no match for a poorly treated malnourished dog's God given scent receptors.

Over the next few weeks after that mission I learned that there were a great number of dogs who either escaped from their harsh captivity or never knew a human being. We had a pack of about fifteen of these wild dogs that roamed the outer perimeter of our Forward Operation Base in the Diyala Province. I often watched these dogs from a safe distance search for anything they could find or bring down to eat. I have no doubt that this pack would kill a human being if an opportunity presented itself.

I was taken with astonishment when I saw a large dog challenge the three-legged Alpha of the pack. I say again the "three-legged" Alpha. To survive the harsh climate and lack of food in Iraq for any dog much less a three-legged dog had to be extremely challenging but let me say this dog was tough. It was a mixed breed of a Saint Bernard and ran it's pack like a true dictator. As soon as the challenger attacked the Alpha the fight was over by the Alpha's counterattack to the challenger's neck. The victor's pack immediately enjoyed the fresh meal. This was just another reminder that I was far from home.

Toward the middle of my tour of duty a single stray dog entered the perimeter of our main gate. He was a white dog but his fur was matted with clods of mud. A name for him immediately came to my mind, "Muddy". Muddy wasn't aggressive like the usual wild pack dogs. What he lacked in aggression he compensated with fear and distress of humans but for whatever the reason after several calm patient attempts Muddy allowed me to softly pet his head. To my knowledge, he never allowed any other U.S. or Iraqi Soldiers to get within three feet of him and my fellow Soldiers referred to Muddy as my dog even though I rarely got to visit with him. He never stayed at our gate for long before he'd wonder off going wherever he'd go and do whatever he did.

Just as all of my other experiences with dogs in Iraq ended in tragedy, my experience with Muddy ended the same. Within the last few weeks I had in Iraq I returned to our main gate to get a shift change briefing from the outgoing Sergeant of the Guard (SOG) and was met with disappointing news. The SOG began his briefing stating that Muddy was dead. He explained that he had gotten wrapped up in concertina (razor) wire and further explained that his Soldiers tried to free him but were unable. The longer I stood there his briefing kept getting worse as he explained that once they couldn't free Muddy, they shot him to ease his suffering then burned his body in place. What a way to start a day in Iraq but after close to a year of riding an emotional rollercoaster not much shocked me at that point.

It was obvious the God gave Muddy a gentle, forgiving spirit. There's no doubt in my mind that his life started out as tragic as it ended and that every day in between was a struggle for mere survival. I'd love to have seen what his life could have been like if he had been born here in the United States.

In Genesis 1:26 we learn that "God said, Let us make man in our image, after our likeness: and let them have dominion over the fish of the sea, and over the fowl of the air, and over the cattle, and over all the earth, and over every creeping thing that creepeth upon the earth". Use Muddy's struggled filled life as motivation to love and appreciate not only your pets but all creatures that are in your care. God entrusted us with great responsibility when He granted us dominion over all the earth and over every creature who lives on it. Just as a child wants to please their parents, lets strive to not let our loving Father down.

Myself and Muddy with SPC Welch in the background

BROTHERS-IN-ARMS

According to the Merriam-Webster dictionary the definition of brothers-in-arms is, a close associate, especially a fellow member of a military service. A gun crew of an M109A6 Paladin consist of four soldiers with assigned duties of driver, cannoneer, gunner, and section chief. The Paladin crew has a sister vehicle crew assigned to a M992A2 Field Artillery Ammunition Supply Vehicle (FAASV) also referred to as the "cat", CAT: Carrier, Ammunition, Tracked. The CAT crew consists of three or more soldiers with the assigned duties of driver, ammunition handler(s), and tracked vehicle commander. These two combat vehicle crews consisting of seven plus soldiers are assigned to a squad in a Field Artillery Battery. Now that you know the Merriam-Webster version of brother-in-arms and what consists of a gun crew, let me tell you about my brothers-in-arms so that you can learn the true meaning.

Other than true family there isn't any sense of family stronger than that of soldiers who form bonds that are made and strengthened through shared blood, sweat, and tears. When soldiers prepare for and serve in combat together, they learn who they are as individuals but more importantly they learn the meaning of a brotherhood like no other. For some, they learn the meaning of family for the first time.

All too often civilians view soldiers as being more than they are but let me fill you in on a little secret. Soldiers aren't extraordinary but very ordinary people that simply do extraordinary things. Soldiers get tired but fight sleep so that others may sleep peacefully. Soldiers struggle with heat, rain, snow, mud, and wind so that others can live in comfort. Soldiers aren't fearless but face their fears. Soldiers lay down their freedoms so that others may be free. Soldiers give their lives so that others may live. Thankfully, soldiers don't do the extraordinary alone but alongside their brothers and sisters-in-arms.

My gun crew was no different. We struggled together in all forms of extreme weather. We laughed, cried, rejoiced, prayed, and bled together. We learned every minute detail of each other. We knew each other's fears, dreams, goals, aspirations, weaknesses, and strengths. We never kicked each other down but always picked each other up. Just like biological brothers if someone messed with one of us, they messed with ALL of us. We always had each other's backs and without hesitation we would gladly lay down our lives for each other. In the thickest fog of war when soldiers question why they were there all it took was a look around to the soldiers serving among us to put us in the right frame of mind. It didn't matter about the political reasons, all that mattered was to get each other home even if it meant we didn't go home ourselves.

John 15:13 reads, "Greater love hath no man than this, that a man lay down his life for his friends." That beautiful Bible verse is a far greater explanation of brothers-in-arms then the Merriam-Webster version and I'm certain that all veterans would agree.

Our Gun Crew at Camp Shelby, MS during pre-mobilization, 2004

Top Left to Right: SPC Jonathan Harrison, SSG Robert Price "Chief", SGT Carl James, SPC Steve Carter, SPC Brad Walker

Bottom Left to Right: SGT Jason "Brother" Berry, SPC Von Reagan, SGT Fred Mize III, SGT "G" Reynaldo Gutierrez Jr.

CRESCENT MOON

The sun had yet to rise when we saw red flashing lights glaring in the morning darkness. The lights grew brighter and brighter as they raced toward our Forward Operation Base (FOB). Once the ambulance began to slow down as it approached our main entrance, I could clearly see its red crescent moon painted on its side.

Everyone placed their weapons at the low ready as the ambulance once again picked up speed in haste toward our main gate's guard station. As soon as the ambulance stopped, U.S. and Iraqi soldiers surrounded it, searched underneath, and inside its patient bay. The driver and EMT cooperated and explained that their patient was an off duty Iraqi soldier who was found on the side of the road with five AK-47 gunshot wounds in his back.

Once I saw the condition of the Iraqi soldier, I quickly escorted the ambulance to the Iraqi Army Hospital located on the Kirkush Military Training Base (KMTB) side of FOB Caldwell. Upon arriving to the entrance to the KMTB hospital, I parked my HMMWV (Humvee) and ran to the back of the ambulance. The ambulance driver met me there while the EMT began preparing the wounded soldier to exit.

I had never seen an Iraqi so pale. Due to loosing so much blood his skin tone was almost as white as mine. I reached for the young soldier as the EMT assisted him to the rear door. He was so weak that he couldn't stand or even lift his head. The EMT placed his lifeless body in my arms and I carried him into the hospital.

Even now, as I reflect on what I witnessed next, tears still fill my eyes. As I cradled and rushed the young man through the front doors, I was dumbfounded to see that the hospital was so dimly lit and no one met us at the door. The ambulance driver and EMT took the lead at that point as we ran down the dark hall way toward the ER. A cold sweat spread across my neck as my stomach fell to my feet once we entered the ER that was manned by one doctor. I gently laid the lifeless soldier onto a cold stainless-steel table and prayed a silent prayer as I slowly backed away hoping to see more people rush to his aid. No one else came.

I looked around and saw nothing but bar shelves surrounding us. I felt sick and defeated as I left the poor excuse for a hospital that was far less adequate than the advanced medical care our U.S. Soldiers were privileged to on our side of the FOB. I swore that as long as I had anything to do with it, I'd never again send anyone, Iraqi or American, into that house of death for medical treatment. I never asked if the Iraqi soldier lived or died but I know his only chance of survival would have taken no less than an absolute miracle from God.

Weeks later, a cold chill broke out across my neck as I saw two crescent moon glad ambulances with red flashing lights rushing toward our FOB. Is this more wounded Iraqi soldiers or could it be a deceitful car bomb attack? The gate one soldiers stopped both ambulances and conducted hasty but careful searches. I inspected both patient bays and saw that they were both chaotically filled with six wounded Iraqi Police Officers who were all badly wounded with AK-47 gunshot wounds to their legs and feet.

Just as with the Iraqi soldier weeks before I quickly escorted the two ambulances onto our FOB but this time would be different. I kept my personal vow, drove past the KMTB hospital, straight to the U.S. Army Medical Station in hopes that these wounded men would receive proper medical care.

The moment I slammed my Humvee in park, three U.S. Army medics rushed to our aid. I assisted with the wounded and found myself once again embracing another injured man in my arms. As I rushed the middle-aged Iraqi Police Officer into our medical station, I saw that his left heal was blown completely off and a thought rushed through my mind. If I wasn't carrying this man, who would be? That random thought, taught me a valuable life lesson which was enforced by God's Holy Word...

Proverbs 16:9

A man's heart deviseth his way: but the LORD directeth his steps.

Proverbs 20:24

Man's goings are of the LORD; how can a man then understand his own way?

There I was serving in Diyala, Iraq, over 6,600 miles away from my home in Strawberry Plains, TN and God loved me enough to teach me a lesson. He taught me that He is in control of my life and directs my steps. I may think that I know what I want out of life or initiate my own plans but He directs my steps.

A year prior to carrying that wounded Iraqi Police Officer in my arms I would have never dreamed that moment would ever take place but God had it planned. Anyone could have helped that man but God desired for me to be there at that moment. I decided to enlist into the Tennessee Army National Guard on October 13, 1999 and God directed our paths to meet in 2005 even though we lived 6,600 miles apart.

No matter our plans for our lives we need to treat everyone we meet with respect, compassion, and love regardless of their race, religion, or creed. We may want to think we're in control but that doesn't change the fact that God divinely directs our steps along the way.

DECEPTION

My favorite President of all time, President Ronald Reagan once said, "Trust but verify." I believe the wise become wise by learning from their mistakes and taking corrective action to no longer make the same mistakes. Even such a wonderful, powerful man such as Ronald Reagan has experienced the pain of deception, the pain of broken trust. He learned to continue to trust but verify.

This too, was a lesson I learned in Operation Iraqi Freedom III. When I first arrived in Iraq, I wasn't naive enough to think for even a moment that I would be able to trust most people in a combat zone where I was viewed as both a foreign invader and a liberator. I never let my guard down when dealing with any Iraqi male to include my several interpreters, the Iraqi Police, and Iraqi soldiers whom served alongside me. I didn't feel this way alone. My entire gun crew knew how tragic the outcome good be if any of us failed to let our guard down.

In December 2004 three Iraqi boys ranging from eleven to thirteen years old arrived at the main gate of our Forward Operation Base (FOB). The boys kindly asked if they could do any work on our base. We asked for their ages and explained that no one under the age of fifteen was authorized to work on the base. They became upset with the news and explained that they had to do something to earn money to support their families because their fathers had been killed in the war and now it was up to them to support their mothers and siblings.

We wanted to help the boys so we hired them to pick up garbage along its outside perimeter. For every bag of garbage, they filled, we paid them one American dollar. At that time, it took 1,170 of their Iraqi dinars to equal one U.S. dollar so these boys were being paid by us far more than they could have ever dreamed of. For over a month day after day the boys returned, picked up garbage and we paid them as agreed. The boys never said much but they won us over due to their dedication and hard work to support their families. I told my family back home about the boys and my aunt Deborah Young, was excited to buy them new shoes.

Then, just as unexpectedly as they appeared at our gate, we saw them taking pictures of our FOB while they were picking up garbage along its perimeter. We immediately detained and questioned them about their actions. Without any hesitation they explained that they had been hired by insurgents for the past couple of weeks to take photos of our buildings where our soldiers were in mass or had little protection from attack. Heartachingly, they further explained that they had given at least three disposable cameras back to the insurgents that hired them, full of photos as they requested. We confiscated their cameras and ordered them to never return.

Once the boys were out of sight from the FOB, we conducted an outer perimeter check and found a chemical mask filter lying beside a freshly dug in mortar position facing our dining facility and refueling area. We learned on that day to, trust but verify.

Me and the boys

SGT James standing in the mortar fighting position

EVERY STEP

Even to this day when I walk across dry, compacted dirt and hear the soft crunch beneath my feet, I'm reminded of the day that I thought was my last. Like so many days spent in Iraq, this one will also forever live in my memory.

The day's mission of enforcing our Forward Operation Base (FOB) Force Protection procedures as the Sergeant of the Guard, was running smooth without any major incidents. Until my Gate 1 guards had a distraught Iraqi civilian taxi driver run to their position and explain that an unknown driver parked his car in the center of their lot and ran off. This report presented a very high likelihood, of one of the worst-case scenarios of attack, by the use of a car bomb. To make matters worse the taxi lot was located 200 yards off the Main Supply Route (MSR) and just twenty-five yards from the entrance to our FOB.

I made the decisions to; lock down the FOB from any incoming and outgoing convoys, had my Force Protection Team cordon off the area surrounding the taxi lot, sent our Quick Reaction Force Team to search for the driver of the car, and radioed for our Air Force Bomb Dog Team to inspect the car. My orders were executed perfectly but several minutes had passed and no Bomb Dog Team. Ten minutes turned to twenty, twenty turned to thirty, thirty to forty-five, forty-five to an hour. Minutes grew longer and my patience grew thinner as I saw a U.S. Army convoy of forty-plus vehicles parked on the MSR needing to enter our FOB. To add to the stressful situation, I had another U.S. Army convoy lined up, prepared to exit our FOB for their assigned mission.

I waited to the point that I couldn't wait any longer because one convoy's mission wasn't getting completed and another convoy could be ambushed at any moment while sitting stranded on the MSR. I knew I had a decision to make. One that no leader wants to ever make. Who's the most trustworthy, capable, and expendable soldier for me to send to inspect the car? It didn't take me long to decide because the answer was always in my heart. All of my fellow soldiers we're completely trustworthy, fully capable, and **none** were "expendable". I would not stand by and watch one of my own die in such a way. So, I made, my decision.

Every step I took toward the car, I knew God heard my prayers over the sound of the dry Iraqi dirt crunching beneath my boots. With every step my heart raced faster and faster as thoughts of my seven-year-old son, Isaiah, rushed through my mind. Will he remember me? Will he be taken care of? The car was getting closer and closer. I could see that I couldn't read the license plate numbers because the plate was folded in half and the backend of the car was squatting. I kept praying and telling myself that they won't waste a car bomb to just kill me. They'd normally detonate car bombs to kill at least four or five soldiers. Why would they kill me alone? I kept walking, step by step, closer and closer.

I can still clearly see the dirt on the passenger side windows as I carefully looked inside for an improvised explosive device (IED), artillery rounds, wiring, or any other signs to clarify the threat. I knew not to open the doors but carefully felt underneath the handles for wiring. Walked to the front of the car and looked underneath the engine. Walked to the driver's side and performed the same search, making my way to the trunk. Once there I got down on my stomach and crawled underneath to inspect the rear end. As I saw copper wiring wrapped around the rear axle, I said aloud, "I'm dead". A few moments (seconds which seemed like hours) past and I realized I was still alive.

I was thankful to rise to my feet but still can't recall walking back to the berm where my fellow soldiers were watching and waiting. My senses must have been so keened up during that moment that I can't for the life of me remember many details after returning to my soldiers and reporting what I saw. All I can remember is that the Bomb Dog Team never arrived, our QRF Team located and detained the driver. He was interrogated over his actions and intentions. Most importantly the car never detonated and we all lived to serve another day.

For years after my return home, anytime I heard a car horn sound up close or far off into the distance, against my will, I was taken back to the moment of taking my first step toward that car. Once there in my mind, feelings of deep emotion rocked throughout my body. I'd feel combinations of anger, sadness, loneliness, and even emotions that I can't find words to explain. These sensations would last for minutes, hours, days, weeks, or even months without ceasing.

None of my military training taught me or prepared me to handle this reaction, this trigger to PTSD. I coped in the best ways I knew and when those ways failed, I coped in ways that were doomed to fail. The only way I could cause the emotions to cease was to spend time with my closest friend Sergeant Jason Berry, AKA, "Brother Berry". Our time together alleviated the confusion and pain. It would clear the fog in my mind but Brother Berry wasn't always around nor could he be.

We all face difficult or even terrible situations in our lives. Most of us have family or friends whom we can turn to during those dark times. But I want to share with you what I've learned in hopes that you turn to the one and only, who can always be there for you when your family or friends cannot. He is the one and only who can heal what pains you. He is the only one who truly understands your pain. His name is Jesus and He's waiting for you to turn to Him. He may answer our prayers in ways that we may not expect nor understand. God, orchestrates His healing through countless ways, which may be through the help of professional counselors, therapist, or pastors. I encourage you to pray without ceasing for Jesus to help you if you suffer from symptoms of PTSD. Be willing to walk through the doors of healing that God opens for you as I have.

DUTY

We as Americans are blessed to have words such as duty, honor, and country engrained in our minds but most importantly we are privileged to have these noble words fill our hearts and inspire our actions from birth till death.

Our beloved service members' unwavering sense of duty is the driving force that causes them to solemnly swear to support and defend the constitution of the United States against all enemies, both foreign and domestic, and bear true faith and allegiance to the same. It is what inspires them to boldly raise their right hand and it is what led far too many of them to give their dying breath to fulfill their solemn oath of enlistment.

Our military's might isn't nor has it ever been technology, training, or tactics but our military's might is the sense of duty that courses through the veins of all who have ever sworn to uphold our nation's values, needs, and freedoms in place of their own. As I train new recruits how to properly wear the United States Army's duty uniform, I ask them a simple question which is, why is U.S. Army on the left side of their uniform and their name on the right? I then proceed to explain the reason being because we as soldiers never place ourselves before the needs of the United States so the U.S. Army is properly placed over our hearts and I tell them to never forget that.

I witnessed firsthand while serving in Operation Iraqi Freedom the monumental difference between U.S. Army Soldiers verses Iraq Army Soldiers because of our understanding and high precedence of duty in our lives. Several times we would stand before a Company formation with fifty plus Iraq Army Soldiers standing before us and select the ones, we needed to take part in that day's missions. We would then witness the cowardice act of multiple Iraqi Soldiers lay their issued AK-47 rifles on the ground at their feet, take off their uniforms down to their boxers and t-shirt, say they quit and walk off our Forward Operation Base seemingly without any shame as though they had done nothing wrong or dishonorable.

The first time we witnessed this we were as dumbfounded as we were furious that these men, these so-called soldiers, weren't willing to do their part in defending their own homeland, their own country, their own people from the insurgence whom we would bravely fight. Myself and my fellow brothers-in-arms were more willing to do whatever was called upon us to do for the betterment and security of the Iraqi people simply because our country whom we dearly loved called upon us to do so. We never quit, we never foundered, we never gave up, all because of our sense of duty, to our country and to each other.

FREEDOM

On 30 January 2005, I witnessed history being made and was beyond thankful to be a part of the moment. On that day I witnessed joy and excitement as much as bravery and courage. For on that day in January the citizens of Iraq experienced the freedom to vote in the parliamentary elections to elect their new National Assembly. Not only did the men of Iraq vote but women alike.

Joy filled the air throughout the Diyala Province and we did all we could to ensure the safety for all who took part and embraced their new freedom. Service men and women all throughout Iraq were on a heightened state of alert because we knew that this new freedom wasn't gained easily and there would be bloodshed to sustain it. All who left the safety of their homes to vote knew this and they bravely filled the voting booths regardless of the threats to their lives.

My gun crew and the other soldiers assigned to that day's Forward Operation Base (FOB) Caldwell Force Protection Team were missioned to conduct security operations throughout the FOB and to conduct check point searches along the main supply route (MSR). Our check point consisted of three Humvee gun trucks and eleven U.S. Soldiers with one Iraqi interpreter. Our mission was to stop every civilian vehicle traveling along the MSR, search for weapons and ask their intent.

Just as any other day in Iraq each vehicle was authorized to have one AK-47 with one 30 round magazine. This may be hard for most Americans to understand but in Iraq this is very minimal to ensure their personal security. For an Iraqi civilian to have an AK-47 in their vehicle is as common as is an East Tennessean to have a hand gun or hunting rifle in their vehicle.

As one can imagine there was a lot of people traveling. During the peak of the day our check point began to get overwhelmed and my ten fellow soldiers became greatly outnumbered. We had several vehicles stopped with car loads of people standing alongside their vehicles waiting to be searched. Even though they understood why we were conducting our searches, tension began to rise. It could be felt like an extra layer of clothing.

Our interpreter was doing all he could to calm the storm, then like a God sent angel an AH-64 Apache Attack Helicopter was seen flying directly toward our checkpoint. No one called for any support. The pilot and gunner must have seen the eleven of us in need of assistance and assistance they certainly gave. I'll never forget making eye contact with the Apache pilot as he and his gunner hovered less than a hundred feet above us, just long enough to get everyone's attention and for the two of us to salute one another to give him clarity that we were good. Once the pilot returned my salute they flew off into the horizon. It was a moment made for Hollywood and one I'll never forget. Needless to say, the God sent angel calmed the storm.

Once we returned to FOB Caldwell, we rejoiced with the Iraqi soldiers as they returned from the security missions and voting themselves. I never saw such happiness on their faces as they proudly showed us their ink stained finger tips as a testament of them pledging their vote. As my children and grandchildren see photos of that day, I'll be able to recall it as it had just happened and know in my heart that I did my small part to make it happen. As I set here and type this memory back to life, I reminisce on the rest of my twenty-years of military service and say that this one day alone made all of my sacrifices worth it. For on that day I did what all soldiers desire to do and that's provide freedom to those who were not free. Praise Jesus, for freedom!

Voting Ballot from 30 JAN 2005

Our M109A6 Paladin at FOB Caldwell, 2005

WELCOME TO
MY NIGHTMARE

◆　◆　◆

On 16 March 2005, I volunteered to assist my good friend, SSG Michael Huskey and 3RD Platoon of A TRP, 1ST Squadron, 278TH Regimental Combat Team, with conducting a dismounted patrol mission in the village of El Mansouria, Iraq. Our convoy left Forward Operation Base Caldwell at approximately 2100. Once we arrived SSG Huskey and I joined the dismounts while our convoy's three Humvee gun trucks and M2 Bradley Infantry Fighting Vehicle stood guard at the village entrance. There was a strange, eerie feel in the air. The only sounds I recall were frogs croaking in the village canals and the dry desert soil crumbling beneath our feet as our platoon crept silently through the village.

SSG Huskey and I were at the rear of the platoon column formation. I was looking to our right flank when approximately fifteen minutes into our patrol our platoon took AK-47 fire from our left flank. Three rounds flew between myself and the medic in front of me, hitting a mudbrick wall. I restrained myself from returning fire because our rules of engagement required us to see our enemy's muzzle flash before returning fire to reduce the risk of civilian casualties.

Our platoon's soldiers who saw the muzzle flash returned fire and our platoon regrouped at our designated rally point.

Our rally point was a cemetery which laid on the far eastern edge of the village. Our platoon leader and radio operator called in a fire mission for three illumination rounds from my own Field Artillery Battery located at Forward Operation Base Caldwell. The situation quickly escalated from bad to worse when the first illumination round lit the black sky and the cemetery into a crimson red as it slowly drifted down to the desert floor. The gunman's position in the village was out of the maximum range of our M109A6 Paladin's 155mm cannons so our cover was blown while his remained in semi darkness.

As I took cover along the cemetery's edge by kneeling down behind a three feet tall mudbrick wall, I looked behind me at SSG Huskey who was laying in an empty, freshly dug grave. The second illumination round lit up the sky above us as SSG Huskey said, "Welcome to my nightmare". Seconds after he spoke those infamous words, the sky itself sounded as though it was being torn apart or ripped into by supernatural means. The thunderous sound grew louder and louder until it ended with an ominous jolt to the ground less than 75 yards from us. Our radio operator called, "cease fire, cease fire" once we realized that the culprit was the third illumination round that didn't disconnect in flight, so the 96 lbs. projectile traveling at one mile per second, plowed through the ground beside us.

Our platoon quickly left the cemetery, took up another column formation and returned to the gunman's last known position to look for his body or detain or neutralize him if he was still a threat. After an hour of searching our platoon was unable to find the gunman and decided to head back to FOB Caldwell before the village grew to an increased unrest.

CLOSING THE DOOR

In a normal way of life people change over time but service in Iraq had a way of radically changing a man in not only a year but in single brief moments. When I arrived in Iraq in 2004, I arrived with an open mind to the differences of my enemy and the culture of the Iraqi people. Due to witnessing countless injustices, hardships, suffering, sexual discrimination, abuse, murders, starvation, destruction, mistrust, disloyalty, manipulation, deception, and acts of war, I was far different from the man I was when I first arrived a year before.

I didn't like the man I became. I felt that hate had taken a strong hold within my heart and mind. I struggled with seeing most Iraqi men as being human. I viewed them as the polar opposite of the Christian values that were instilled in my heart. I didn't want to return home as a man ingulfed with hatred, but I only had two weeks to shed the hate that was filling my soul. I prayed to God to guide and lead me in His ways so that I could lay down the overwhelming burden that I bore.

As He always does, He answered my prayer for His will to be done. He placed it on my heart to spend my remaining free time with my Iraqi interpreters and share my Christian beliefs and values with them. For any of you who are reading this and have been to or have served in Iraq know that sharing Christian beliefs and values with several devout Muslims may be a daunting if not dangerous feat. But I was willing, and God was able.

The next day I spoke with each of my interpreters and asked if I could visit with them over the next two weeks, alone in their tent after my duty was complete. I didn't realize it then, but I do now as I'm writing this, just how unusually easy it was for us to agree to meet and share our religious beliefs and values with each other. We simply agreed to meet peacefully and to maintain that peace regardless of our beliefs or different world views.

Just as we agreed over the next two weeks we met in their tent. Although it was against my military training, I met them alone, yet still armed of course. God gave me such a peace and comfort with every moment of our fellowship. I want you to know that I'm not choosing to use the word "fellowship" lightly for our meetings were true fellowship. We enjoyed pure meaningful deep conversations with each other. We ate together. We laughed and even cried together. I read to them the Holy Bible and they read to me the Quran. We spoke freely and frankly. In the end we became friends and together we closed the door to hatred.

I don't want to mislead anyone to think that when I returned home that I didn't have any hate or disdain in my heart for the experiences I endured because that would be far from the truth. I returned home a changed man, in many ways a better man. I became appreciative of every meal and for every morning that I wake. I became thankful for both clean and hot water. I became thankful for the astonishing beauty of East Tennessee. Still to this day every morning before my feet hit the floor, I thank God for the air I breathe and for sand not being underneath my feet.

I'm now thankful for the man I became through the woven experiences of serving with my brothers-in-arms. I realize, I'm still a work in progress regarding overcoming the effects of PTSD but overcome them I will through the power and will of God. I'm a simple man but more importantly I'm a born-again child of God and He cares for His children.

FIGHT ON

"Only the dead have seen the end of war."

- Plato

Plato's quote is validated every time men faceoff in combat and any survive. There are countless service men and women who bear the scars of war but all scars aren't visible by the eyes alone. Some scars are so deep, so painful that those who bear them feel ashamed to show anyone their wounds. Rather than face the possibility of being judged or misunderstood for their actions that left them so wounded they suppress their memories into the deepest chasms of their souls.

Just as the wounded cry out for a medic on the battlefield, I encourage anyone who suffers with symptoms of PTSD, depression, and/or anxiety to seek help. Your fight should not be fought alone and can certainly be won.

For over nine years I internally fought my battles with PTSD and depression but finally reached out for help by sharing my pain with my friend Bruce Davenport. With his help I was able to overcome one of my main PTSD triggers that I thought would never heal. This was a major turning point in my life because I learned that I wasn't forever broken. I could be healed and I had a choice. For the first time, I felt an empowerment over my symptoms. With Bruce's help I won a major battle, but my war with PTSD wasn't over.

Several years later many of my symptoms crept back into my life and rather than try to cope and face them alone I decided to seek help once again. This time, I sought counseling and met with Mr. Jamie Suarez a Counselor who understood my pain, never seemed to judge me or get tired of hearing me vent my pain from the past, nor my frustrations of the present. I had weekly sessions with Jamie from September 2018 through March 2019 at which point I felt as complete and calm as I had in quite some time.

Five months later I realized that I was again having major struggles with concentrating even to the point that I was forgetting how to do certain simple everyday tasks. I wasn't retaining or comprehending conversations with my wife, coworkers, friends, or my pastor's sermons.

One month later, while driving for five hours with a fellow soldier and friend, SFC Daniel Finstad, I made the following mistakes all in the same day; drove through a red light, almost rear ended a tractor trailer, drove past two exits that I meant to take, took a wrong turn and drove up the wrong side of the road. After this I knew I had a serious problem and reached for help once again.

This time, I contacted Jesse James, who's the Behavioral Health Consultant for the Tennessee Army National Guard and a fellow serving Soldier in the same. Jesse, wisely put me on a ninety-day driving profile limiting me to driving no more than thirty minutes from my home. He also recommended that I met with Tony Weaver, who's the Military Services Program Clinical Counselor at Helen Ross McNabb Center in Knoxville, TN.

My time with Tony Weaver helped to not only improve my overall quality of life but God used him to open my eyes to see what I was missing by allowing my symptoms to cloud my focus for today and dreams for tomorrow. As I write this book my therapy sessions with Tony Weaver are still taking place.

My war isn't yet over and I accept that it may never be but just as a trained and disciplined soldier, I fight on with the help of my family, friends, therapists, and Jesus Christ. My battles have strengthened my faith and relationship with God and if that's the reason for God allowing my symptoms to take their place in my life than I'll be forever thankful. My symptoms alone aren't who I am but my battles with them have molded me into the man I am today.

As this humble book comes to an end my life's story will continue. I'll remain steadfast in my faith that God will continue to walk with me and lead me in His ways, just as He has thus far throughout my life. If you don't have a true relationship with Jesus Christ, nor know Him as your LORD and savior I pray above all that you pray for Him to come into your life and accept Him as your savior from the punishment of your sins. For there is no decision more important that you'll ever make in your life. For this one decision will have an eternal, everlasting effect.

Those who helped me along my way...

Bruce Davenport
Former Guidance Counselor & "Beloved Friend"
Jefferson County High School
115 W. Dumplin Valley Road
Dandridge, TN 37725

Jamie Suarez, Counselor, LPC, MHSP, MS
Cokesbury Counseling Center
2025 Castaic Lane
Knoxville, TN 37932

Jesse James, Ph. D, LPC, MHSP
Behavioral Health Consultant
Tennessee Army National Guard
Contractor, Hoskins & Co.
2109 Army Drive
Louisville, TN 37777
(865) 985-4894
Jesse.a.james40.ch@mail.mil

Tony Weaver, MA
Military Services Program Clinical Counselor
Helen Ross McNabb Center
3712 Middlebrook Pike
Knoxville, TN 37921
(865) 444-2333 x2633
Tony.weaver@mcnabb.org

FLIGHT OUT

Standing in wait to be airlifted out of Forward Operation Base Caldwell was a very exciting yet sobering moment. I stood alongside SSG Robert Price "Chief" waiting for our chalk's CH-47 Chinook helicopters to land and fly us out together. While we stood there together on that cool Iraq night, I couldn't help but remember crossing the border into Iraq with him, just shy of a year prior. I pondered on all that we experienced throughout our tour of duty and wondered what the rest of our lives would be like once we returned home and what would come of the Iraqi soldiers and interpreters whom we cared about once we were gone.

I can still hear the thunderous roar of our mighty CH-47 Chinook's twin engines and tandem rotors as they landed for our pickup. As we boarded the Chinook, I was thankful to be one of the last soldiers onboard because it gave me one of the two prized seats closest to the rear bay loading ramp. During the flight, our crew chief manned a M240 machine gun while sitting on the open loading ramp. That was my first night flight in a Chinook and I quickly learned that our zero light flight operation was going to be an exciting one.

As we pushed toward our destination of the Balad Airbase located in the Sunni Triangle near Balad, Iraq, our

Chinook flew at its top speed of 196 MPH while constantly flying up and down to avoid being targeted by Rocket Propelled Grenades (RPG). Soon after our flight began, anxiety took hold in my gut not because of fear of being shot down from the sky by an RPG but because our Chinook was raining hydraulic fluid upon us throughout the cargo bay. I yelled out to our crew chief to ensure he was aware of the problem. He calmly replied to me, "Don't worry about it Sarge, it's only a problem if it stops leaking". I was dumbfounded yet comforted at the same time.

Upon arriving to Balad Airbase our travels would soon take place in an even mightier and far larger aircraft, the breathtaking, Boeing C-17 Globemaster. Myself, Chief, and my good friend SPC Mark Patton were absolutely amazed by the sheer size of the C-17's seemingly endless wingspan and cargo bay. I was thankful to being flown out of Iraq and back to Camp Buehring, Kuwait in such an awesome aircraft.

My last memory in Iraq took place walking beside Chief while boarding the mighty bird. He looked me square in my eyes and said one word, "Spit". At first, I didn't understand where he was going with this and he again spoke the single word, "Spit" then I realized. Just as my left boot made contact with the massive C-17's cargo bay door, while my right boot was still planted on the Iraq earth beneath me, I spat on the tarmac and entered the plane. I didn't spit on Iraq as a whole nor on my service to my country. I spat on all the injustices we witnessed, on all the hate that fueled our enemy, on all the disdain shared by our enemy for our Christian and American values, and on the fog of war that still clouds so many minds.

I'm thankful for my service to our beloved country. I'm thankful to have done my part in defending our country's values and needs. Most importantly I'm thankful to have done my small part to provide freedom to others. Like so many soldiers before us, we may never fully understand all of the reasons for sending us to war but that isn't our place. We weren't politicians or the Commander-in-Chief. We were soldiers called to service and serve we did. Soldiers don't choose their missions but they certainly choose how they'll serve. For the soldiers of 1ST Howitzer Battery 278TH Regimental Combat Team, I can attest, that they served by giving our country and Iraq their very best. For that, I'll always be thankful to have served among them.

Our Brave and Noble Iraqi Interpreters

Members of the best gun section
ever to serve in the Tennessee Army
National Guard

SSG Robert Price "Chief"

SPC Brad Walker

SPC Brandon Welch

SGT Jason "Brother" Berry and myself

SGT Carl James

SPC Von Reagan

SPC Steve Carter

SPC Jonathan Harrison

SGT "G" Reynaldo Gutierrez Jr.

Soldiers of the New Iraqi Army who
served alongside us

SPC Mark Patton with Iraqi Army Soldiers

An Iraqi Soldier holding my M-4 Rifle

Iraqi Soldiers standing guard

Let us remember those members of the Tennessee Army National Guard, who gave their all...

John 15:13

Greater love hath no man that this, that a man lay down his life for his friends.

SGT Paul W. Thomason III

KIA when a roadside bomb detonated near
his heavy equipment truck in a supply convoy
outside of Kirkuk, Iraq on 20 March 2005

SFC Stephen C. Kennedy

KIA while on patrol by small-arms fire when attacked by enemy forces in Balad Ruz, Iraq on 04 April 2005

SGT Alfred B. Siler

Died when his HMMWV "Humvee" hit
another vehicle in Tuz, Iraq on 25 May 2005

SSG Mark O. Edwards

Died from a non-combat related cause at his
forward operation base near Tuz,
Iraq on 09 June 2005

SSG Asbury F. Hawn II

KIA by hostile fire while on a mounted patrol near FOB Bernstein, Iraq on 13 August 2005

SGT Shannon D. Taylor

KIA while on a mounted patrol when attacked
by hostile fire near FOB Bernstein,
Iraq on 13 August 2005

SGT Gary L. Reese Jr.

KIA while on a mounted patrol when attacked
by hostile fire near FOB Bernstein,
Iraq on 13 August 2005

SSG Victoir P. Lieurance

KIA when a roadside bomb detonated near his
HMMWV "Humvee" during patrol operations
in Samarra, Iraq on 22 August 2005

SGT Joseph D. Hunt

KIA when a roadside bomb detonated near his
HMMWV "Humvee" during patrol operations
in Samarra, Iraq on 22 August 2005

SGT Robert W. Tucker

KIA when a roadside bomb detonated near his
HMMWV "Humvee" during patrol operations
in Dujail, Iraq on 13 October 2005

REFERENCES

Bushatz, A. (n.d.). National K9 Veterans Day. Retrieved from https://www.military.com/veterans-day/k9-veterans-day. html.

U.S. pet ownership statistics. (n.d.). Retrieved from https://www.avma.org/resources-tools/reports-statistics/us-pet-ownership-statistics.

ABOUT THE AUTHOR

Fred C. Mize III, is a Master Sergeant in the Tennessee Army National Guard and has honorably served his state and country for over twenty years. Above all, he's most thankful for his salvation given to him by Jesus Christ and for his beautiful wife Hollea, their children, and grand-children. God has placed it on his heart to help others with their battles with PTSD, depression, and anxiety. He prays that this book will help and encourage those in need to seek professional help and most importantly Jesus Christ, for He is the truth and the life.

Made in the USA
Monee, IL
18 July 2021

73427962R00066